WHAT'S IT WORTH?

A Straight-Talk Guide to Selling Your Business and Exiting Like a Winner

MICHAEL TOUPS

What's It Worth?

Copyright ©2026 by Michael Toups

All Rights Reserved

No part of this publication may be reproduced, distributed, or transmitted in any form or by any means, including photocopying, recording, or other electronic or mechanical methods, without the prior written permission of the author, except in the case of brief quotations used in reviews or other permitted uses under copyright law.

This book is provided for informational purposes only. The views expressed are solely those of the author and are not intended to constitute legal, tax, accounting, financial, or investment advice. Readers should consult qualified professionals before making any business, financial, or legal decisions.

Published by Crossfin LLC.

For more information visit: *www.WhatsItWorthConsult.com*

Library of Congress Control Number: 2026905941

ISBN: 979-8-234-02061-1 (Paperback)
ISBN: 979-8-234-02062-8 (e-book)

Printed in the United States of America

DEDICATION

To my wife, for her love, steadfast support,
and faith-filled strength.

And to the spouses of entrepreneurs who understand
the true cost of building a dream.

Table of Contents

CHAPTER 1
Begin with the End in Mind   1
    1.1 — What Does "The End" Actually Look Like?   2
    1.2 — Two Types of Sellers   3
    1.3 — Why Buyers Pay More for "Planning"   4
    1.4 — The "Sellability Score": How Ready Are You?   5
    1.5 — The 3 Big Outcomes You Must Decide Early   5
    1.6 — The Exit Timeline (Simple but Real)   7
    1.7 — The Owner's Biggest Blind Spot: "I'm the Business"   8
    1.8 — A Simple "Begin with the End" Exit Action Plan   8

CHAPTER 2
Who Can I Trust?   13
    2.1 — The "Selling a Business Team" (In Plain English)   14
    2.2 — What Each Professional Actually Does (And Why)   15
    2.3 — The "Trust Test": How to Choose the Right People   18
    2.4 — Warning Signs (A.K.A. "Run")   19
    2.5 — The Right Questions to Ask Before You Hire Anyone   20
    2.6 — The Most Important Hire: Your Intermediary   21
    2.7 — How to Know You Found the "Right One" (Intermediary)   22

Chapter 3
Surviving Due Diligence   25
    3.1 — What Due Diligence Really Is (In Plain English)   26
    3.2 — The Three Levels of Due Diligence   28
    3.3 — Why Deals Die in Due Diligence   29
    3.4 — The Golden Rule of Due Diligence   30
    3.5 — What a Buyer Will Ask For (The Real Checklist)   31
    3.6 — The Due Diligence Data Room (Your New Best Friend)   33
    3.7 — How to Handle Due Diligence Requests Like a Pro   34
    3.8 — The Buyer Will "Find Issues." Don't Panic.   35
    3.9 — How to Protect Yourself (Do Your Own Due Dilligence)   36

Chapter 4
Numbers Don't Lie   39
    4.1 — The Two Financial Versions of Every Business   40
    4.2 — Your Financials Are Your Business Reputation   41
    4.3 — What Buyers REALLY Look At   42
    4.4 — SDE vs EBITDA (The No-BS Explanation)   42
    4.5 — The Most Important Documents in Your Entire Sale   44
    4.6 — Your "Financial Story" Must Be Consistent   45
    4.7 — Pro Forma Financials: Powerful or Dangerous   46
    4.8 — Add-Backs: The Easiest Way to Lose Credibility   47
    4.9 — What "Clean Books" Actually Means   48
    4.10 — The Simple Financial Improvements That Raise Value Fast   48

Chapter 5
Beauty is in the Eye of the Beholder   51
    5.1 — The Most Common Seller Mistake: "My Business Is Special"   52

5.2 — The Four "Value Drivers" Buyers Pay Up For 52

5.3 — Valuation is NOT Just a Multiple 53

5.4 — The 3 Most Common Valuation Methods 53

5.5 — What a Buyer Will Pay Extra For (Premium Value) 55

5.6 — What LOWERS Value (Even if Revenue is High) 56

5.7 — Strategic Buyer vs Financial Buyer (The Fork in the Road) 56

5.8 — The Most Important Valuation Skill: Setting Expectations 58

5.9 — The "Reality Check" Valuation Range 58

5.10 — Your Business Might Be Worth More Than You Think… 59

Chapter 6
Art of the Deal 61

6.1 — The Biggest Negotiation Mistake Sellers Make 62

6.2 — The "Offer" Is Not the Offer 63

6.3 — The 7 Most Important Deal Terms (Besides Price) 63

6.4 — Negotiation Is a Process, Not a Moment 67

6.5 — The Golden Rule of Negotiation 68

6.6 — The Superpower: Buyer Competition 68

6.7 — How to Handle Lowball Offers (Without Losing Your Mind) 69

6.8 — Avoid This Trap: "I Just Want This Over With" 70

6.9 — The Most Important Negotiation Skill: (Non-Negotiables) 70

Chapter 7
The Buyer Isn't Buying Your Business… They're Buying Confidence 73

7.1 — The Buyer's Inner Monologue (Spoiler: It's Terrified) 74

7.2 — There Are Only Two Types of Businesses 75

7.3 — The Confidence Equation 76

7.4 — What Buyers Pay Premium Multiples For 77

7.5 — The #1 Buyer Fear: Owner Dependency — 77
7.6 — Buyers Don't Want Potential. They Want Predictability. — 78
7.7 — The "Confidence Presentation" Position Your Business — 79
7.8 — The Buyer's "Trust Scorecard" — 79
7.9 — The "Confidence Builder Kit" (Easy Wins) — 80
7.10 — The Real "Secret" to Premium Offers — 81

CHAPTER 8
Deal Killers (and How to Avoid Them) — 85
8.1 — Most Deal Killers Are Not "Big Problems" — 86
8.2 — The Top 10 Deal Killers (and How to Fix Them) — 87
8.3 — "Closing Creep" Can Be a Deal Killer — 93
8.4 — The "Prevention Plan": Build a Deal-Proof Business — 93
8.5 — Quick "Deal Risk Scoreboard" (Simple for Buyers and Sellers) — 94

CHAPTER 9
Cash in Your Pocket — 97
9.1 — The Sale Price Illusion — 98
9.2 — The "Net Proceeds" Formula (What You Actually Keep) — 99
9.3 — The 7 Biggest Things That Reduce Cash in Your Pocket — 100
9.4 — Asset Sale vs Stock Sale — 103
9.5 — Allocation of Purchase Price (Hidden Tax Weapon) — 104
9.6 — The "Cash at Close" Mindset — 105
9.7 — The Closing Statement: Where Reality Shows Up — 105
9.8 — After the Sale: Don't Blow It — 106

Chapter 10
What's My Why? — 109

- 10.1 — The Big Surprise After the Sale: "Now What?" — 110
- 10.2 — The Real Reasons People Sell (And All of Them Are Valid) — 111
- 10.3 — The Seller Identity Problem (Nobody Warns You About) — 112
- 10.4 — The 4 Paths After You Sell — 112
- 10.5 — Giving Back: The Highest ROI You'll Ever Get — 115
- 10.6 — The "Perfect Exit" Isn't Necessarily the Perfect Deal — 116
- 10.7 — Your Post-Sale Plan (The Practical Version) — 116
- 10.8 — The Final Truth: You're Not Selling Your Business — 117

Appendix
Exit Action Plan Summary — 121

About the Author — 127

Chapter 1

Begin with the End in Mind

"The best way to predict the future is to create it."
— Peter Drucker

Let's start with the uncomfortable truth:

Most business owners don't plan to sell their business. They *hope* to sell it.

Hope is not a strategy. Hope is what you do when you can't find your keys and you're already late.

If you want to sell your business for top dollar (or even just "fair dollar"), you need to start with a clear picture of the end result. Not just *selling* but selling well.

Selling a business isn't like selling a used truck. You can't just wipe it down, take a few flattering pictures, post it online, and say, "Runs great, only driven to church on Sundays."

A business sale is more like preparing a home for a tough buyer with a sharp inspector, a suspicious spouse, and a mortgage lender who assumes everyone is lying.

The good news?

If you start preparing early, you control the story, the valuation, and the final outcome.

The even better news?

You don't have to become a corporate finance expert or Wall Street guru to do it.

You just need a plan and that starts by beginning with the end in mind.

1.1 — What Does "The End" Actually Look Like?

Before you talk about price, you need to define the destination.

Too many owners say:

- "I want to sell."
- "I want to cash out."
- "I want to retire."
- "I'm tired."

All valid but none of these explain what you want your life to look like **after** the deal.

Ask yourself these three simple questions:

1. What does "enough money" mean for me?
2. What am I walking away from?
3. What am I walking toward?

Here's the shocker: Some owners sell their business, get the money… and then feel lost.

They spent 20 years building the business and about 20 minutes planning what comes next. So, the "end" isn't just a sales price.

The end is:

- your financial future
- your freedom
- your identity
- your peace of mind
- your family goals
- your legacy

Planning for what comes next matters in how the deal is structured.

1.2 — Two Types of Sellers

There are usually two kinds of people who sell their business:

Type A: The Builder

This owner says:

"I'm going to sell in 3–5 years."

- they plan
- they prepare
- they create systems
- they build management
- they reduce risks
- they clean up the financials

These owners often get premium offers because buyers can *"touch and feel"* **the structure.**

Type B: The Burner

This owner says:

"I can't take it anymore. I'm done."

Maybe they're exhausted. Maybe there's a health issue. Maybe there's family drama. Maybe business is slipping.

But now they're selling under pressure and buyers love pressure. Pressure makes sellers negotiate against themselves. This doesn't make the seller weak, it makes the seller human.

If you want to avoid selling like The Burner, you need to start thinking like The Builder today… Even if you're not selling for years.

1.3 — Why Buyers Pay More for "Planning"

Buyers don't pay more for "potential." They pay more for **certainty**.

Let's make this simple and sum up the buyer's logic in one sentence:

"If I buy this business, will it keep making money without the owner?"

If the answer is *maybe*, buyers get nervous and nervous buyers don't pay top dollar. They:

- lower offers
- demand earnouts
- push seller financing
- request ridiculous holdbacks
- "find problems" during due diligence

They become… creative and you want to avoid that.

That's why early planning increases value because it makes the business more predictable.

1.4 — The "Sellability Score": How Ready Are You?

Here's a simple Sellability Score self-test. Rate each item 1–10.

	Category	Question	Score (1–10)
a.	Financials	Are your statements clean and accurate?	___
b.	Ownership Dependency	Can the business run without you?	___
c.	Customer Risk	Is revenue spread across customers?	___
d.	Systems	Do you have documented processes?	___
e.	Team	Do you have leadership beyond you?	___
f.	Contracts	Do you have solid customer/vendor contracts?	___
g.	Compliance	Are licenses, insurance, HR files updated?	___
h.	Growth	Is revenue stable or increasing?	___
i.	Market Position	Is your brand credible and defensible?	___
j.	Documentation	Can you prove everything you claim?	___

Total Score:

- **80–100** = highly sellable / strong valuation potential
- **60–79** = sellable but risk-adjusted (expect negotiations)
- **40–59** = sellable but discounted (earnouts likely)
- **Below 40** = "buyer will smell fear"

(Yes, buyers can smell fear. They don't even need to be in the room.)

1.5 — The 3 Big Outcomes You Must Decide Early

Most people think selling a business is about picking a buyer. Actually, it's about picking an outcome.

The three most common outcomes are:

Outcome #1: Cash Out

You want:

- the most money
- the cleanest exit
- the fastest closing
- minimal involvement afterward

This is the dream scenario, but it requires the highest level of preparation, because buyers will only pay "cash out money" for low-risk businesses.

Outcome #2: Partial Exit

You sell some equity, keep some. This works well when:

- the business is growing
- you still enjoy part of it
- you want liquidity but not full retirement
- the buyer wants you to stay involved

This can be a great wealth-building move, but it also means you're still in a relationship with the buyer.

However, this business relationship can be a lot like dating: Exciting in the beginning… complicated later.

Outcome #3: Legacy Transition

You want:

- to protect employees
- to preserve the business name
- to prioritize community impact
- to ensure continuity
- to exit in a way you feel proud of

Often seen with:

- family businesses
- local service companies
- restaurants
- mission-driven companies

Legacy transitions can still be profitable, but the "best buyer" isn't always the highest bidder.

1.6 — The Exit Timeline (Simple but Real)

Here is the reality of a typical business sales timeline:

Preparation Phase	Marketing & Buyer Search	Due Diligence / Close
|---------------------|	|---------------------|	|---------------------|
6–24 months	3–9 months	2–6 months

Translation: If you want a smooth exit, you ideally begin preparing **12–24 months** before you want to sell. Not because it takes that long to list the business but because it takes that long to fix what buyers punish:

- messy financials
- undocumented processes
- shaky contracts
- owner dependency

- customer concentration
- weak leadership bench

And here's the truth:

You don't rise to the level of your goals. You fall to the level of your preparation.

1.7 — The Owner's Biggest Blind Spot: "I'm the Business"

Many owners build great companies, but they accidentally build them like this:

- the owner sells
- the owner manages
- the owner handles operations
- the owner handles relationships
- the owner approves everything

And after 15 years, they wake up and realize:

The business is profitable… but it's not sellable.

Because the owner isn't just the CEO…the owner is the operating system. Buyers don't want to buy an operating system that lives in someone's head.

Buyers want a business that runs like a machine, not a business that runs like a heroic daily rescue mission.

1.8 — A Simple "Begin with the End" Exit Action Plan

You don't need a 90-page strategic plan. You need a clear action plan.

Here's your practical Exit Action Plan Starter Kit:

Step 1: Decide your target exit date

- Even if it's rough: "Spring 20xx."

Step 2: Decide the type of sale you want

- cash out
- partial exit
- legacy sale

Step 3: Define what "success" looks like (example)

- "Net $5M after taxes"
- "No earnout"
- "Business stays in the community"
- "My top employees are protected"

Step 4: Start removing owner dependency (today)

- delegate approvals
- build SOPs
- appoint a #2 leader and build a team
- document relationships and processes

Step 5: Clean financials (Now! – Not Later)

(We'll cover that more deeply in Chapter 4.)

Step 6: Identify deal blockers (weaknesses)

Make a list of weaknesses you already know:

- customer concentration
- outdated contracts
- lack of clear reporting
- pending lawsuits
- "handshake agreements"
- no lease assignment clauses

Don't panic. Just list them.

What gets measured can get fixed.

Chapter 1 Summary — Begin with the End in Mind

"By failing to prepare, you are preparing to fail."
— Benjamin Franklin

Action Plan: No More Excuses

To get started, complete these 7 steps:

1. Write down your target exit year
2. Decide whether you want cash out, earnout, partial exit, or combination
3. Estimate your "number" (how much you want after taxes)
4. Identify the 3 biggest risks in your business
5. List what only YOU do today
6. Choose 1 task to delegate immediately
7. Commit to treating your business like an asset — not a job

Because once you begin with the end in mind… You stop running the business like it's your identity and you start building it like it's a product someone would actually buy.

Up Next: Chapter 2 — Who Can I Trust?

We'll talk about building the right team:

1. Attorney (Transaction / M&A Attorney)
2. CPA / Accountant
3. Personal Financial Advisor (Wealth Manager)
4. Professional Intermediary (Business Broker or M&A Advisor)

…and how to avoid the kind of "help" that costs you time and money.

Chapter 2

Who Can I Trust?

"Trust is the glue of life. It's the most essential ingredient in effective communication. It's the foundational principle that holds all relationships."
— STEPHEN R. COVEY

Let's be honest. When you decide to sell your business, *everybody* suddenly becomes your best friend. People you haven't heard from in 10 years will pop up like:

- "Hey buddy! Heard you might be selling…"
- "I know a guy who buys businesses…"
- "My cousin does M&A…"
- "I can get you top dollar."

Somewhere in the middle of all that noise is one very serious question:

Who can I trust?

Because selling a business is one of the biggest financial events of your life. You are about to turn 10, 20, maybe 30 years of sweat into a check (or a structured payout, which is code for: *not all the cash at once*).

And here's the thing:

- A great team can increase your valuation, protect your deal, and help you sleep at night.
- A bad team can cost you hundreds of thousands… and you don't even know it.

This chapter is about building the right professional team, understanding each role, and most importantly how to avoid hiring the wrong people.

2.1 — The "Selling a Business Team" (In Plain English)

When you sell a business, you're not just picking one professional.

You're assembling a deal team.

Think of it like putting together a championship team:

- Not everyone plays the same position
- You don't want your kicker trying to play quarterback
- And you definitely don't want the guy who "watched a YouTube video" acting as your coach

Your core team should include:

1. Attorney (Transaction / M&A Attorney)
2. CPA / Accountant
3. Personal Financial Advisor (Wealth Manager)
4. Professional Intermediary (Business Broker or M&A Advisor)

Depending on your business size and complexity, you may also add:

- insurance specialist
- tax attorney
- valuation analyst

- estate planning attorney
- CFO consultant

But the core team are your four main pillars.

2.2 — What Each Professional Actually Does (And Why)
1) Your Attorney — The Risk Blocker

Your attorney:

- drafts/reviews contracts
- negotiates legal terms
- helps you avoid getting trapped in "gotcha" clauses
- protects you if things go sideways later

Best analogy: Your attorney is your seatbelt *and* airbag. Hopefully you never need them… but if you do, you REALLY do.

What you want in an attorney:

- experience in business sale transactions
- not just "general business law"
- understands deal structure, indemnities, earnouts
- doesn't panic under pressure

What you don't want:

- an attorney who treats your business sale like a traffic ticket
- someone who argues for sport
- someone who bills hours without moving the ball forward

2) Your CPA / Accountant — The Truth Teller

Your CPA / Accountant:

- ensures financial statements are accurate
- helps normalize the numbers (add-backs, one-time expenses)
- prepares tax returns
- helps defend your financial story during buyer review

Best analogy: Your CPA / Accountant is your lie detector.

Not because you're lying, but because buyers assume everyone is lying. Buyers are professional skeptics, and they should be. They'll be paying you big money.

What you want:

- clean bookkeeping and accurate financials
- knowledge of business sale preparation
- ability to produce reports quickly
- confidence when challenged

What you don't want:

- "We can get that later" energy
- missing reconciliations
- tax returns filed late
- can't explain your numbers in plain English

3) Your Personal Financial Advisor — The Life Planner

Your personal financial advisor / wealth manager:

- plans what happens after the sale
- helps you invest the proceeds wisely

- plans retirement / second career runway
- helps reduce financial stress and avoid big mistakes

Best analogy: Your Personal Financial Advisor is like a guard rail on a mountain road.

Because here's what nobody tells business owners:

You can sell your business the right way… and still run out of money.

That happens more often than people admit. Suddenly you've got cash and freedom, but:

- no plan
- too much emotion
- bad advice from friends
- shiny new investment "opportunities" (aka traps)

What you want:

- fiduciary mindset (client first)
- experience working with business owners
- tax-aware planning
- calm, disciplined approach

What you don't want:

- someone who sells products instead of advice
- someone who gets paid for transactions, not outcomes
- someone who can't explain fees clearly

4) Your Professional Intermediary - The Deal Maker

This is the person most owners misunderstand. A professional intermediary can be a:

- **Business Broker** (smaller deals)
- **M&A Advisor** (larger deals)

Their job is to:

- position your business for maximum value
- find qualified buyers
- create a buying process (competition = higher price)
- manage negotiations
- keep you emotionally stable (this is an actual value)

Best analogy: Your intermediary is your real estate agent for your business… except the inspections are harder and the buyers are scarier.

They also act as your:

- shield
- hype-man
- gatekeeper
- problem-solver
- therapist with a spreadsheet

If you choose the right one, they more than pay for themselves with a better deal.

2.3 — The "Trust Test": How to Choose the Right People

Let's make this simple. To *accept* team members, they should pass this test:

The 6 Trust Filters ("ACCEPT")

1. <u>Alignment</u> — Do they prioritize your desired outcome?
2. <u>Competence</u> — Do they actually do this for a living?
3. <u>Clarity</u> — Can they explain things simply without hiding behind jargon?
4. <u>Experience</u> — How many deals have they done?

5. <u>Proof</u> — Can they show results and references?
6. <u>Transparency</u> — Do they explain fees, timelines, and risks clearly?

If any one of these is missing, pause until you find a team you can *accept*.

2.4 — Warning Signs (A.K.A. "Run")

Here are the biggest red flags when hiring professionals for your sale:

Red Flag #1: They promise a price too early

If someone says: "I can get you $10 million easy" …before reviewing anything?

That's not confidence. That's a sales pitch.

Professionals don't guess. They validate.

Red Flag #2: They talk more than they ask

A good advisor asks:

- your goals
- your stress points
- your timeline
- your weaknesses
- your deal-breakers

A bad one just talks. And talks. And talks. Usually about themselves.

Red Flag #3: They make your sale about them

Beware the "hero advisor" who acts like: "You're lucky to have me."

You're not hiring a savior. You're hiring a service provider.

Red Flag #4: They avoid specifics

If you ask:

- "How do you get buyers?"
- "How many deals like mine have you closed?"
- "What will your process look like?"

... and they respond with vague fluff? Not good.

Red Flag #5: They pressure you

Pressure kills judgment.

A real professional won't rush you. They'll guide you.

2.5 — The Right Questions to Ask Before You Hire Anyone

Here's the checklist. Use this like you're interviewing for a high-level executive position... because that's what you're doing.

Questions for your Attorney:

1. How many business sales have you handled?
2. Do you handle asset sales and stock sales?
3. What deal terms cause the most risk?
4. What does your billing typically look like?

Questions for your CPA / Accountant:

1. Can you support add-backs and normalization?
2. Can you respond quickly during due diligence?
3. How do you help defend financial quality?

Questions for your Financial Advisor:

1. Are you a fiduciary 100% of the time?
2. How do you help clients after a liquidity event?
3. What's the plan to protect the money?
4. What's your fee structure?

Questions for your Intermediary:

1. How many deals have you closed?
2. How many were in my industry or size range?
3. What's your process from listing to closing?
4. How do you confidentially market my business?
5. How do you screen buyers?
6. What's your fee structure? (and what's included)
7. What common issues stop deals from closing?
8. How will you help defend my valuation?

2.6 — The Most Important Hire: Your Intermediary

The Intermediary you choose will shape your entire sale outcome.

A strong intermediary:

- creates buyer competition
- protects confidentiality
- prepares your narrative
- prevents emotional mistakes
- keeps deals alive during chaos

A weak intermediary:

- lists you everywhere like a garage sale
- attracts unqualified buyers
- loses control of the process
- lets buyers dictate terms
- causes deals to die

In other words… Your intermediary is not just a salesperson. They are your deal architect. Choose wisely!

2.7 — How to Know You Found the "Right One" (Intermediary)

When you meet the right intermediary, you'll notice:

- they talk about risk before price
- they identify weaknesses without insulting you
- they have a process (not a "shotgun" approach)
- they understand deal structure
- they set expectations
- they don't oversell
- they can show real proof of past closings
- they make you feel calm, not hyped

Hype doesn't close deals. Preparation closes deals.

Chapter 2 Summary: Who Can I Trust?

"The naive believe everything, but the shrewd watch their steps."
— *The Book of Proverbs 14:15*

Selling your business is a major life event. Don't try to do it with:

- your cousin's attorney
- your friend's CPA who "can probably handle it"
- a broker who lists donut shops and car washes but has never sold a company like yours
- a financial advisor who starts talking about annuities before asking about your goals

Instead... Build a trusted team of specialists who:

- protect you
- validate your numbers
- maximize value
- guide your decisions
- keep the deal alive

Action Plan: Build the Team Before You Need the Team

- Identify 2–3 candidates for each core role (Attorney, CPA, Advisor, Intermediary)
- Interview them using the questions above
- Ask for references
- Choose your intermediary carefully, because they will drive the process

Up Next: Chapter 3 — Surviving Due Diligence

In Chapter 3, we'll talk about what due diligence really is (hint: it's not friendly), what buyers demand, and how to prepare so you don't get blindsided.

Because due diligence isn't just a phase in the process.

It's the buyer's chance to beat you up, and your job to stand tall and proud because you're prepared.

Chapter 3

Surviving Due Diligence

"Trust, but verify."
— Ronald Reagan

If selling your business is the wedding, then due diligence is the part where your future spouse hands you a clipboard and says: "Before we get married, I'd like to review your entire past… in detail… with receipts."

And if you think that sounds dramatic, welcome to due diligence.

Due diligence is where buyers go from:

- **excited** → "This could be a great acquisition!" to…
- **suspicious** → "What if this is a beautiful dumpster fire?"

It is the single most stressful phase of a business sale for most owners because it feels personal.

They ask about:

- your money
- your systems
- your contracts

- your tax returns
- your employees
- your customer relationships
- your legal exposure
- your insurance
- and yes… occasionally your soul

And they do it in a way that makes you feel like you're being audited by an emotionally detached robot.

Here's the key mindset shift: Due diligence is not an insult. It is the buyer doing their job. Your job is to survive it without:

- panicking
- getting defensive
- losing control of the deal
- or accidentally talking your buyer out of buying

This chapter will help you do exactly that.

3.1 — What Due Diligence Really Is (In Plain English)

Due diligence is the buyer's process of verifying:

- everything you claimed
- everything they assumed
- and everything they're afraid of

Buyers are asking one question:

"Is this business worth what I'm paying… and will it keep working after I own it?"

Due diligence focuses on two things:

1. Proof

Can you prove:

- revenue
- margins
- growth
- contracts
- equipment ownership
- compliance
- client retention
- intellectual property

2. Risk

Can the buyer avoid:

- lawsuits
- payroll issues
- tax exposure
- customer loss
- hidden debt
- weird obligations
- owner dependency

If proof is weak and risk is high, buyers start doing something you never want: They start rewriting the deal. Lower price, more holdbacks, earnouts, seller financing… you name it.

If proof is strong and risk is low, the deal closes smoothly.

3.2 — The Three Levels of Due Diligence

Due diligence is not one thing. It's usually three tracks happening at once:

Level 1: Financial

- financial statements
- tax returns
- bank statements
- payroll reports
- AR/AP aging

Level 2: Legal

- contracts
- leases
- employee agreements
- litigation history
- insurance
- compliance and licenses

Level 3: Operational

- SOPs (standard operating procedures)
- systems and processes
- customer concentration
- vendor dependencies
- equipment
- IT systems
- management and staffing

You may have one buyer or an entire squad of specialists:

- analyst
- CPA
- attorney
- banker
- insurance rep
- operations manager

And every one of them has questions. So, it can start feeling overwhelming fast.

3.3 — Why Deals Die in Due Diligence

Let's not sugarcoat it: Most deals don't die because the buyer doesn't like the business. They die because:

- the seller can't produce documents
- the numbers don't match the story
- risk shows up unexpectedly
- trust gets damaged
- the process becomes chaotic

Due diligence is where optimism collides with reality and reality wins.

The top 10 deal killers during due diligence:

1. Missing or incomplete financials
2. Tax returns don't match financial statements
3. Customer concentration is worse than disclosed
4. Contracts are verbal / informal
5. Unrecorded liabilities (loans, refunds, warranties)

6. Lease issues or non-transferable lease terms
7. Employee issues (misclassification, missing documentation)
8. Key vendor dependency
9. Owner does everything
10. "Surprise problems" (lawsuits, liens, compliance failures)

Notice something important: None of these are mean the business is bad, just undocumented which creates uncertainty.

Buyers don't pay big money for uncertainty.

3.4 — The Golden Rule of Due Diligence

Here it is. Memorize this:

The buyer doesn't want your answers. They want your proof.

Anybody can say:

- "We're profitable"
- "Our customers love us"
- "We have long-term relationships"
- "We're growing"

Due diligence is where the buyer says: "Great. Show me."

And if you respond with:

- "It's in my head"
- "I'll have to find it"
- "We don't really track that"
- "My accountant has it somewhere"

The buyer hears: "This is a risk."

So, the goal is simple: Make due diligence boring.

- Boring due diligence closes deals.
- Chaotic due diligence creates price drops.

3.5 — What a Buyer Will Ask For (The Real Checklist)

Below is a simplified due diligence list. This is the stuff buyers almost always request.

Financial Documents

- last 3–5 years tax returns
- year-to-date P&L and balance sheet
- monthly P&Ls for last 12–24 months
- bank statements (selected months)
- AR aging report
- AP aging report
- list of loans/debt
- owner add-backs breakdown

Sales / Revenue Proof

- top customers list
- revenue by customer
- signed contracts (if applicable)
- customer churn/retention
- pipeline report (if you have one)

Legal & Compliance

- entity documents (articles, operating agreement)
- contracts and agreements
- insurance policies
- litigation history
- licenses, permits
- sales tax filings (if applicable)
- worker comp coverage

HR / Employee

- org chart
- employee roster (roles, pay, start date)
- contractor list
- employee handbook (if any)
- benefit plans and obligations

Operations

- SOPs (even basic ones)
- inventory process
- vendor agreements
- equipment list
- IT systems list
- access list (software subscriptions)

This sounds like a lot because it is.

But here's the trick: You don't have to do it alone.

Your intermediary and CPA/accountant should help you build the diligence package and respond to requests efficiently.

3.6 — The Due Diligence Data Room (Your New Best Friend)

If you're serious about selling, you need a data room.

A data room is just an organized file system where everything lives:

- Google Drive
- Dropbox
- OneDrive
- a secure data room platform

Think of it as the business equivalent of cleaning your house before guests arrive.

Except the guests are paying millions and bring flashlights.

A simple data room folder structure:

    01 – Financials
    02 – Tax Returns
    03 – Customers & Sales
    04 – Contracts
    05 – Employees
    06 – Insurance
    07 – Legal / Entity Docs
    08 – Operations
    09 – IT / Systems
    10 – Real Estate / Lease

If your data room is clean:

- trust increases
- buyer confidence increases
- deal closes faster
- price stays stronger

If your data room is messy:

- buyer gets nervous
- buyer thinks you're hiding something
- buyer finds "problems"
- buyer starts discounting value

3.7 — How to Handle Due Diligence Requests Like a Pro

Here's the best advice in this whole chapter:

Do not respond emotionally. Respond professionally.

Due diligence requests can feel annoying: "Why do you need THAT?"

Because they're spending real money. That's why!

Best practices:

- respond quickly (within 24–48 hours whenever possible)
- provide complete documents
- label files clearly
- never upload messy drafts or incomplete statements
- keep communication centralized through your intermediary

And here's the secret:

When you respond fast and organized, the buyer starts thinking: "This seller is professional. This business is real."

You become trustworthy by behavior and preparation. Not by words.

3.8 — The Buyer Will "Find Issues." Don't Panic.

During due diligence, buyers WILL find issues.

- Sometimes they're real issues.
- Sometimes they're buyer anxiety.
- Sometimes they're negotiation tactics.

So, expect this: The buyer might say:

- "We're concerned about your customer concentration."
- "We noticed margins dipped last year."
- "We need more clarity on your add-backs."
- "We discovered some outdated contracts."

Here's what you **don't** do:

- Argue
- get offended
- say "that's none of your business"
- act like they're accusing you of fraud

Here's what you **do**:

- clarify calmly
- provide documentation
- demonstrate controls and solutions
- show how the risk is handled

The goal is not to be perfect... The goal is to be credible.

3.9 — How to Protect Yourself (Do Your Own Dilligence)

This book is seller-focused, but you still need basic protection:

Make sure you have:

- **signed NDA** before sharing sensitive info
- buyer has shown proof of funds / financing capability
- controlled access to your data room
- clear process for Q&A
- no direct buyer access to employees/customers without agreement

You do not want your:

- competitors
- tire-kickers
- or "I'm just curious" people learning your secrets.

A professional intermediary helps prevent this.

Chapter 3 Summary — Due Diligence Rewards the Prepared

"Whoever walks honestly walks securely, but one whose ways are crooked will fare badly.."— *The Book of Proverbs 10:9*

If you remember one thing from this chapter: Due diligence is a test of trust.

And the winners are the sellers who are:

- trustworthy
- organized
- transparent
- calm
- prepared
- fast

It's not about having no flaws. It's about having no surprises.

Because surprises lower value.

Action Plan: Due Diligence Prep

- Create your data room (basic folder structure above)
- Upload last 3 years of tax returns
- Upload last 2 years of financial statements
- Pull your top customer list by revenue
- Gather all major contracts
- Create a basic equipment list
- Create an employee roster (name, role, pay, start date)
- Identify your 3 biggest business risks before the buyer does

Up Next: Chapter 4 — Numbers Don't Lie

In Chapter 4, we'll get into financials in a clean, simple way:

- how buyers read your statements
- why tax returns matter so much
- and how the wrong numbers can cost you *real money*.

Because in a business sale, you don't get paid for your effort.

You get paid for your proof.

Chapter 4

Numbers Don't Lie

"In God we trust. All others must bring data."
— W. Edwards Deming

Let's get something straight right away: Buyers don't buy your story…

They buy your numbers.

You can have the most inspiring business journey on earth:

- started with $400 and a dream
- worked nights and weekends
- built a loyal customer base
- survived COVID, inflation, labor shortages, and that one employee who "quit" but kept showing up

All impressive, but a buyer looks at your business the same way a banker looks at a loan application: "Show me the numbers."

Because the numbers answer the only question that matters:

Will this business make money after I own it?

- If your financials are strong, clean, and credible? You win.
- If your financials are messy, inconsistent, or "creative"? You lose.

And "lose" in this case means:

- lower valuation
- harsher deal terms
- longer due diligence
- more holdback
- earnouts
- seller notes
- or the deal dies entirely

So, yes… numbers don't lie.

But owners sometimes do (accidentally or not). Not necessarily out of dishonesty, but out of habit (because sometimes they've lied to themselves).

4.1 — The Two Financial Versions of Every Business

Every business has two versions of its financial picture:

Version 1: The Owner Version

This version includes things like:

- your truck payment
- your "business dinners"
- your cellphone plan
- your home office setup
- that "marketing expense" that was actually a family vacation with one client lunch

It's normal. Owners run perks through the business. It's not evil. It's not rare.

But buyers want to see something different.

Version 2: The Buyer Version

This version answers:

- what does the business earn *without* owner extras?
- what does it cost to replace the owner?
- what is the true profit of the company?

That's why we normalize financials. Not to fake the numbers, but to clarify them.

4.2 — Your Financials Are Your Business Reputation

Here's a truth that might sting: The quality of your financial statements reflects the maturity of your business.

Clean financials send a message:

- "This is a real company."
- "This owner runs a tight ship."
- "You can trust what you're buying."

Messy financials send a different message:

- "This business runs on vibes."
- "There may be hidden problems."
- "If they can't track money… what else can't they track?"

Buyers do not reward chaos. They punish it.

4.3 — What Buyers REALLY Look At

Most business owners think buyers focus on:

- gross revenue
- number of employees
- how long you've been in business

Those things matter… but they're not the core.

Buyers focus on these 5 things:

1. Revenue consistency
2. Profitability
3. Cash flow
4. Owner dependency
5. Risk

In financial terms, they're hunting for one key metric: <u>EARNINGS.</u>

Meaning: The true economic benefit is what the business generates.

For small businesses, that's often measured as:

- **SDE** (Seller's Discretionary Earnings), or
- **EBITDA** (Earnings Before Interest, Taxes, Depreciation, and Amortization)

4.4 — SDE vs EBITDA (The No-BS Explanation)

SDE (common in small business sales)

SDE is basically:

Net Profit (plus)

  + add-backs (discretionary owner perks)

+ owner compensation

+ certain one-time expenses

+ non-cash expenses (amortization and depreciation)

+ interest

+ income taxes

SDE (Seller's Discretionary Earnings)

It answers: "How much benefit does the owner get from the business each year?"

SDE is common for:

- small owner-operated companies, considered "Main Street"
- businesses under ~$5M sale price (not always, but often)
- typically has a lower earnings multiple for valuation than EBITDA

EBITDA (common in larger deals)

EBITDA is Earnings Before Interest, Taxes, Depreciation and Amortization

It's your operating profit before taxes, debt structure, and certain non-cash accounting expenses.

With EBITDA, buyers are no longer calculating what one working owner can pull out. They are measuring the operating performance of the business itself, assuming professional management.

It answers: "How profitable is the business as an operation, independent of ownership structure?"

EBITDA is common for:

- larger businesses, considered Middle Market
- companies with management teams, so you normalize excess owner's comp
- acquisitions by private equity or strategic buyers

Example: $1 million in Net Income

SDE Valuation	EBITDA Valuation
• Net Income: $1,000,000 • Owner's Compensation: $270,000 • Income Taxes: $300,000 • Interest: $80,000 • Depreciation/Amortization: $150,000 • Discretionary/One-time: $65,000 **SDE = $1,864,000**	• Net Income: $1,000,000 • Excess Owner's Comp: $70,000 • Income Taxes: $300,000 • Interest: $80,000 • Depreciation & Amortization: $150,000 • Discretionary/One-time: $65,000 **EBITDA = $1,665,000**

EBITDA is lower because we assume a paid professional manager replaces the owner.

Valuation Difference:

Main Street - SDE multiple (est. 3x):
$1.864M × 3 = ~$5.6M

Lower Middle Market - EBITDA multiple (est. 5x):
$1.665M × 5 = ~$8.3M

- SDE businesses are valued on what the owner can take home.
- EBITDA businesses are valued on scalable, transferable earnings and get a higher multiple.

4.5 — The Most Important Documents in Your Entire Sale

If you want to sell a business, you need to know this:

Buyers believe <u>tax returns</u> more than P&Ls.

Every. Single. Time. Because tax returns are filed under penalty of perjury.

A P&L can be printed in 30 seconds.

So, here's the Buyer's Trust Hierarchy

- Tax returns (highest trust)
- Bank statements
- Payroll reports
- Financial statements prepared by CPA

How to lose trust…

- "Here's my QuickBooks summary"
- "I made a spreadsheet"
- "Trust me, bro" (Not an accounting term but widely understood.)

4.6 — Your "Financial Story" Must Be Consistent

Consistency is everything. If the buyer sees:

- revenue on tax return = $3.8M
- revenue on P&L = $4.4M
- revenue in your pitch deck = $5.1M

The buyer will <u>not</u> say: "Wow, he's doing even better than expected!"

The buyer will say: "What is going on here?"

Once the buyer's trust breaks, the price drop follows.

Rule: Your financial story must match across:

- financial statements
- tax returns
- bank activity
- customer contracts

It doesn't have to be perfect, but it must be explainable.

4.7 — Pro Forma Financials: Powerful or Dangerous

A pro forma is basically: "Here's what the business *could* look like under certain assumptions."

They can be helpful… but they can also be hilarious.

Some business owners build pro formas like: "We'll triple revenue next year, cut all expenses, and hire unicorns who work for free."

Buyers aren't dumb.

Pro formas don't increase price unless:

- assumptions are realistic
- there's proof behind the model
- you can show how growth is achieved

A good pro forma includes:

- historical baseline (actuals)
- realistic assumptions
- specific growth drivers
- capacity/staffing plan
- marketing/sales plan
- margin logic

A bad pro forma includes:

- dreams
- vibes
- prayers
- wishful thinking with Excel formatting

Buyers can smell fantasy numbers.

4.8 — Add-Backs: The Easiest Way to Lose Credibility

Add-backs are the seller's adjustments to show: "These expenses won't exist under new ownership."

- Some add-backs are legit.
- Some are... comedy.

Legit add-backs

- one-time legal expense
- owner's personal travel not needed
- owner salary (if buyer will replace owner differently)
- one-time equipment purchase
- unusual or nonrecurring expenses

Not-so-legit add-backs

- normal repairs
- standard marketing costs
- employee overtime that happens every year
- sales-related expenses

Rule:

If you want an add-back accepted, you must show:

- documentation
- explanation
- consistency
- why it will not recur

The goal is not to inflate... it's to clarify.

4.9 — What "Clean Books" Actually Means

When an intermediary says: "Your books need to be clean."

They don't mean: "Your QuickBooks need to be neat."

They mean:

Clean books = credible books

Credible books include:

- consistent chart of accounts
- reconciled accounts monthly
- clear separation of personal vs business expenses
- clean payroll reports
- supporting documents stored and accessible
- good categorization of expenses
- accurate balance sheet

If your balance sheet and P&L are a mystery novel… buyers will not finish reading it.

They'll just walk away.

4.10 — The Simple Financial Improvements That Raise Value Fast

Here are 7 things that raise value quickly:

"High Impact" improvements

1. Reconcile books monthly (not yearly)
2. Reduce cash payments / undocumented transactions

3. Track revenue by customer consistently
4. Create clear expense categories
5. Document add-backs properly
6. Produce monthly financial packets
7. Keep financial and tax documents together

Just doing these basic things can increase value because buyers reward professionalism.

Chapter 4 Summary — Numbers Don't Lie

"It's not personal… it's business."
— *The Godfather*

Your Business Is Worth What Your Financials Can Prove.

A buyer is not paying for your effort. They're paying for:

- earnings
- proof
- stability
- confidence

Numbers are the language of confidence.

Action Plan: Financial Prep Checklist

- Pull last 3 years of tax returns
- Pull year-to-date P&L and balance sheet
- Create monthly P&L statements for last 12–24 months
- Create a clear add-backs list with documentation
- Identify financial inconsistencies before the buyer does

- Clean up personal expenses in business accounts
- Talk with your CPA/accountant about normalization and SDE/EBITDA view

Up Next: Chapter 5 — Beauty is in the Eye of the Beholder

In Chapter 5, we'll cover valuation and pricing, including:

- different valuation methods
- why buyers pay more for certain businesses
- and how to set a realistic target without scaring buyers away

Business valuation isn't just math… it's psychology.

Chapter 5

Beauty is in the Eye of the Beholder

"Price is what you pay. Value is what you get."
— Warren Buffett

Let's start with a hard truth that will save you from pain:

Your business is not worth what you *think* it's worth.

It's worth what a qualified buyer is willing to pay… under real deal terms… after due diligence… on a Tuesday… when they're in a good mood.

And yes, valuation is part math, but it's also part psychology.

Because business value is like real estate:

- Two houses on the same street can sell for wildly different prices.
- Same square footage. Same layout.
- One sells in 3 days above asking.
- The other sits for 6 months while the owner says, "I don't get it. It's a great house!"

In business sales, that happens constantly.

That's why this chapter matters. This is where we talk about how value is set realistically without getting emotionally attached to a number.

5.1 — The Most Common Seller Mistake: "My Business Is Special"

It's normal to feel this way:

- you built it
- you sacrificed for it
- you solved problems nobody else could solve
- you survived the chaos

So of course, it feels special to you, but buyers don't give value to sentiment.

They value:

- cash flow
- stability
- growth potential
- risk level
- transferability

Here's the buyer mindset: "Can this business run and profit without this owner?"

- If yes → higher valuation
- If no → lower valuation

So yes… beauty is in the eye of the beholder, and the beholder is the buyer.

5.2 — The Four "Value Drivers" Buyers Pay Up For

Want a higher valuation?

Great. Then focus on what buyers actually pay for.

Buyers will pay a premium for:

1. **Strong earnings**
2. **Stable revenue**
3. **Low risk**
4. **Transferability (business runs without you)**

You can't negotiate your way out of weak fundamentals. You can only build your way out.

5.3 — Valuation is NOT Just a Multiple

Most owners hear something like: "Businesses sell for 3–5x earnings."

Then they do quick math and think: "Perfect! I'll be retired by Labor Day."

But multiples are not magic… they reflect risk.

The multiple is basically a buyer saying: "How confident am I that these earnings will continue?"

- Higher confidence → higher multiple
- Lower confidence → lower multiple

So, your job is to increase buyer confidence.

5.4 — The 3 Most Common Valuation Methods

(There are many methods, but these are the big three.)

Method 1: Multiple of Earnings (Most Common)

This is the most common for small and mid-sized business sales.

Usually based on:

- SDE multiple (small owner-operated)
- EBITDA multiple (larger deals)

Example:
If EBITDA is $1,000,000
and the multiple is 5x
Valuation = **$5,000,000**

Simple but not always easy.

Method 2: Asset-Based Valuation

This is used when the business is worth more for what it owns than what it earns.

Common in:

- heavy equipment businesses
- manufacturing
- distressed companies
- asset-rich service companies

Example:
Equipment: $900K
Inventory: $400K
Receivables: $300K
Less liabilities: -$200K
Estimated asset value: **$1.4M**

Asset method is often a "floor value," not the full story.

Method 3: Discounted Cash Flow (DCF)

DCF is more common in corporate finance.

It asks: What is this future cash flow worth today?

It requires assumptions:

- future growth
- future margins
- discount rate (risk factor)

DCF can be useful, but for many business owners it's like: "Let me estimate the future using math and optimism."

So, buyers usually rely more on earnings multiples unless the deal is larger.

5.5 — What a Buyer Will Pay Extra For (Premium Value)

There are certain traits that get premium valuation.

Premium business characteristics

- recurring revenue (subscriptions, contracts)
- diversified customer base
- solid management team (not owner-dependent)
- documented SOPs
- consistent margins
- strong reviews/reputation
- long-term customer relationships
- low competition niche
- transferable systems (not owner-dependent)

If you have these traits, you can expect stronger offers.

5.6 — What LOWERS Value (Even if Revenue is High)

Here's the part nobody likes, but everybody needs to know:

Value killers

- customer concentration (1–3 customers = most revenue)
- owner dependency
- inconsistent financials
- poor documentation
- declining trendline
- too many handshake deals
- legal or compliance issues
- weak middle management
- unreliable vendors

If a buyer sees these, they don't just lower the price. They change the structure and request:

- earnouts
- holdbacks
- seller notes
- longer transition requirements

Value Killers mean: You don't actually "cash out." You cash out later… maybe.

5.7 — Strategic Buyer vs Financial Buyer (The Fork in the Road)

Not all buyers will value your business the same way.

In fact, two buyers could value your company very differently.

Strategic Buyer

This is a company that buys you because it fits their strategic goals.

They might value:

- your customer base
- your brand
- your location
- your team
- your capabilities
- your market entry advantage

Strategic buyers often pay more because they're not just buying earnings… they're buying your advantages.

Financial Buyer

This buyer values your business mainly as a cash-flow asset.

They focus on:

- financial performance
- operational structure
- risk controls
- scalability

They can still pay well, but their valuation is more formula-driven.

Strong structure and consistent earnings matter most.

Key takeaway:

A strong intermediary helps you position your business to the right buyer type.

Selling to the wrong type is like trying to sell ice cream to Eskimos.

5.8 — The Most Important Valuation Skill: Setting Expectations

Here's what many owners don't realize: Pricing too high is not "ambitious." It's expensive because:

- qualified buyers won't engage
- time on market increases
- your business looks stale
- buyers assume something's wrong
- you attract lowballers and tire-kickers

Worst case? The market trains buyers to expect you'll drop the price.

So, now you're negotiating from weakness.

That's why realistic valuation isn't pessimism… it's strategy.

5.9 — The "Reality Check" Valuation Range

This is a helpful mindset: Stop chasing "the number."

Build a valuation range. (example)

- low case: $4.5M
- expected case: $5.3M
- premium case: $6.2M

Then ask: What would need to be true to earn the premium case?

- stronger contracts
- less customer concentration
- cleaner books
- management team
- improved margins

Which means valuation becomes a target you can build toward.

5.10 — Your Business Might Be Worth More Than You Think…

Here's the good news: Some businesses sell for premium valuations not because they're huge but because they're:

- clean
- consistent
- documented
- transferable
- low-drama

Buyers will pay for peace. A predictable business is a valuable business.

Chapter 5 Summary — Beauty is in the Eye of the Beholder

"A thing is worth what someone is willing to pay for it."
— *Publilius Syrus, Roman Philosopher*

Value Is a Mix of Math and Confidence

Valuation isn't just "earnings x multiple." It's:

- earnings quality
- risk level
- transferability
- buyer type
- deal environment

The biggest lever you control is <u>buyer confidence.</u>

Because businesses don't sell for what you say, but what you can prove.

Action Plan: Valuation Prep Checklist

- Get a baseline valuation range from your intermediary
- Identify what buyer type would pay most for your business
- List the top 5 value drivers in your company
- List the top 3 risk drivers lowering your multiple
- Decide what's realistic vs what's emotional
- Work with your CPA/accountant to calculate real SDE/EBITDA
- Strengthen documentation and contracts to raise confidence

Up Next: Chapter 6 — Art of the Deal

In Chapter 6, we'll talk about negotiations, including:

- handling buyers
- controlling the process
- protecting your leverage
- and making sure you don't "win the negotiation" and lose the deal

The goal isn't the negotiations themselves, it's too close.

Chapter 6

Art of the Deal

"Let us never negotiate out of fear.
But let us never fear to negotiate."
— John F. Kennedy

Negotiation is where business owners get into trouble. Not because they're bad negotiators but because they're emotional negotiators.

If you're selling a business you built from scratch, emotion is unavoidable. This isn't like selling an extra office chair on Facebook Marketplace. This is your life's work.

So, when a buyer starts pushing you around, nitpicking your numbers, or "suggesting adjustments," what happens? You start feeling:

- offended
- defensive
- anxious
- impatient
- argumentative

This chapter will help you negotiate like a professional, not like someone fighting over the last chicken wing at a family barbecue.

Because the Art of the Deal is not about:

- being the toughest person in the room
- "winning" every point
- crushing the buyer

The Art of the Deal is about one thing:

Protecting value while keeping the buyer moving forward.

6.1 — The Biggest Negotiation Mistake Sellers Make

"Sellers negotiate price before negotiating the *deal structure*."

Price is only one line item.

Structure is the difference between:

- **money now**
  vs
- **money later**
  vs
- **money maybe**

You can sell for $6M and end up with $3.5M.

Or sell for $5M and net $4.7M.

How?... Structure.

Before you get excited about a big number, you need to understand what you're actually agreeing to.

6.2 — The "Offer" Is Not the Offer

Buyers often present an offer that looks clean.

Then due diligence happens and suddenly:

- "We need an earnout"
- "We need you to finance part of the deal"
- "We need a holdback"
- "We need to adjust working capital"
- "We need a reduction due to risk"

It's like ordering a steak and getting the bill later like:

"Steak was $60… but the restaurant ambiance charge was another $60."

So understand this now:

The LOI (Letter of Intent) is a proposal, not a promise.

It's the beginning of negotiation, not the end.

6.3 — The 7 Most Important Deal Terms (Besides Price)

If you remember nothing else from this chapter, remember these terms.

Key deal terms every seller must understand:

1. **Cash at Close**
2. **Earnout**
3. **Seller Note**
4. **Holdback / Escrow**
5. **Working Capital Adjustment**
6. **Non-Compete / Non-Solicit**
7. **Transition Period & Employment Requirements**

Let's break them down quickly.

1. Cash at Close

This is the good stuff!

This is what most sellers mean when they say: "I want to cash out."

You want as much cash at closing as possible. Because cash at close is:

- real
- immediate
- not dependent on future performance
- not dependent on buyer mood swings

2. Earnout

Earnout means:

"You'll get paid additional money later if the business hits performance goals."

Earnouts can be fair, but they can also be:

- confusing
- hard to control
- easy to manipulate
- emotionally exhausting

Earnouts are where sellers go from: "I sold my business!"

to: "I'm still in this thing… but now I have less control."

Earnout = risk transferred to the seller.

3. Seller Note

This means you loan money to the buyer. Example:

- Price: $5M
- Buyer pays $4M at closing
- $1M is a seller note paid over 3–5 years

Seller notes can be okay, but make sure:

- interest rate is fair
- security/collateral exists if possible
- default terms are clear
- personal guarantee if appropriate

Because a seller note is you saying: "I believe in this buyer enough to finance them."

That belief better be backed by proof.

4. Holdback / Escrow

Buyer holds money back temporarily for risk. Example:

$250K held in escrow for 12 months for indemnities.

This is common, but it should be:

- reasonable in size
- limited in time
- clear release terms
- not "forever money"

5. Working Capital Adjustment

This is the silent killer. This is where sellers get blindsided.

Working capital is basically:

- accounts receivable
- inventory
- accounts payable
- cash needed to run business

Buyers want enough working capital so the business can operate immediately after closing.

Totally fair, but this must be clearly defined. If it isn't you'll get hit at closing with:

"We're reducing the purchase price due to working capital deficiency."

Translation: A last-minute haircut.

6. Non-Compete / Non-Solicit

Most deals include non-competes.

Reason: Buyer wants to protect the investment, but non-competes must be:

- reasonable
- clear in duration
- tied to consideration
- enforceable in your state

Also watch out for:

- non-compete that blocks you from working at all
- non-solicit language covering everybody you've ever met

7. Transition Period

Most buyers require transition support:

- training
- introductions to customers/vendors
- system handoffs

Common transition structures:

- 30–90 days included
- then paid consulting after

If the buyer wants you "employed" for 1–3 years, you need to decide:

Are you selling a business…or applying for a job?

6.4 — Negotiation Is a Process, Not a Moment

Most sellers think negotiation is: "We go back and forth and finally agree."

In reality, negotiation is more like:

The 4-stage negotiation flow

1. **Positioning**
2. **Process Control**
3. **Term Management**
4. **Closing Push**

Your intermediary (broker/M&A advisor) should manage this, because if you negotiate alone, you may do this:

- talk too much
- reveal your bottom line
- react emotionally
- lose leverage

- "concede" too early
- create doubt in the buyer

Owners are too close to it. That's why you need a pro.

6.5 — The Golden Rule of Negotiation

"The party who controls the process controls the deal."

Control the process by:

- setting deadlines
- having multiple buyers
- keeping communication structured
- responding quickly
- staying organized

When sellers lose process control, buyers start dictating terms.

6.6 — The Superpower: Buyer Competition

Want leverage? Get at least two potential buyers.

One buyer = buyer has power
Two buyers = seller has power
Three buyers = buyers start acting right

Competition creates:

- urgency
- improved terms
- higher price
- fewer ridiculous requests

It's not personal. It's economics.

This is why strong intermediaries build buyer pipelines and run a controlled process.

6.7 — How to Handle Lowball Offers (Without Losing Your Mind)

Lowball offers happen. Sometimes because:

- buyer is fishing
- buyer doesn't understand value
- buyer is broke
- buyer is testing you

Rule #1: Don't take it personally.

Rule #2: Don't negotiate with unserious people for too long.

A professional intermediary will usually respond with:

- clarification questions
- a counteroffer anchored in reality
- firm boundaries

Best response strategy:

"We appreciate your offer. Based on earnings and risk profile, we're targeting $X–$Y. If you can move into that range, we're happy to continue discussions."

Notice that:

- you don't insult them
- you don't argue
- you don't sound desperate

You sound like a real company.

6.8 — Avoid This Trap: "I Just Want This Over With"

This is when sellers destroy their own valuation.

- Deal fatigue kicks in.
- The buyer drags due diligence out.
- The seller gets exhausted.

Then one day the seller says: "Fine. Whatever. Just close."

That moment can cost you:

- At least 10% - 20% of the purchase price
- or worse: unfavorable terms you regret for years

If you feel fatigue, don't negotiate. - Delegate.

Let your intermediary manage the chaos because tired sellers negotiate poorly.

6.9 — The Most Important Negotiation Skill: (Non-Negotiables)

Before negotiations begin, you must define:

Your "Must-Haves" - Examples:

- minimum price
- minimum cash at close
- no earnout
- max transition period
- no personal guarantee on anything
- no non-compete longer than X years

Your "Nice-to-Haves" - Examples:

- keeping brand name
- employee retention protections

- seller note with high interest
- consulting agreement

If you don't define these in advance, you'll define them emotionally in real time.

That's dangerous.

Chapter 6 Summary — Art of the Deal

"**In business, you don't get what you deserve. You get what you negotiate.**"
— Dr. Chester L. Karrass

Negotiate Terms Like a Pro, Not Like a Tired Owner

Negotiation isn't about being aggressive. It's about being:

- structured
- calm
- patient
- strategic
- protected

The best sellers don't negotiate everything… They negotiate the important things. They protect:

- price
- structure
- risk
- transition obligations

Avoid the biggest trap: Winning the argument but losing the deal.

Action Plan: Negotiation Prep Checklist

- Define your minimum acceptable terms (price + structure)
- Create your non-negotiables list
- Make sure your intermediary is running a controlled buyer process
- Avoid single-buyer negotiations if possible
- Prepare for common buyer tactics (push for earnout, holdback, working capital)
- Decide in advance how long you're willing to stay post-close

Up Next: Chapter 7 — The Buyer Isn't Buying Your Business… They're Buying Confidence

In Chapter 7, we'll talk about the buyer mindset:

- what scares buyers
- what makes them pay more
- what makes them walk away
- and how to make your business feel like a safe bet

Confidence is the currency that drives premium valuations.

Chapter 7

The Buyer Isn't Buying Your Business... They're Buying Confidence

"Risk comes from not knowing what you're doing."
— Warren Buffet

Let's say you're selling your house. Two homes are for sale on the same street:

- Same size
- Same layout
- Same neighborhood
- Same price

But one house looks like:

- clean kitchen
- fresh paint
- new roof
- organized paperwork
- polite seller

The other looks like:

- mystery stains
- 42 unfinished projects
- receipts everywhere
- "Yeah, the roof leaks sometimes but it's fine"

Even if both houses are technically "the same," which one gets the better offer?

That's what buyers do with businesses.

The buyer is not buying your business... They're buying certainty.

They're buying:

- a smooth transition
- predictable earnings
- reliable systems
- manageable risk
- stable customers
- clean documentation
- leadership continuity

In one word? Confidence.

This chapter is about how buyers think, what makes them nervous, and how to position your business to diffuse risk so buyers feel safe paying top dollar.

Premium valuations don't come from hype... They come from confidence.

7.1 — The Buyer's Inner Monologue (Spoiler: It's Terrified)

Business buyers are optimistic... but cautious. Even when they love the business, they're thinking:

- "What don't I know yet?"
- "Is the seller hiding something?"
- "Will customers leave after the owner exits?"
- "Are the financials real?"
- "Are employees going to quit?"
- "Am I buying a machine… or a mess?"

Buyers aren't just doing due diligence. They're doing fear management.

So, the best sellers do something smart: They make the buyer feel safe. Not through words but through proof and process.

7.2 — There Are Only Two Types of Businesses

From a buyer's perspective, there are two categories:

Type 1: A Business with real operations, including:

- systems
- people
- reporting
- documentation
- structure

This business can be transferred. This business can be scaled.

Type 2: An Owner With a Job

This looks like a business on paper… but really it's:

- the owner is sales
- the owner is operations

- the owner is quality control
- the owner is customer service
- the owner is accounts receivable collections
- the owner is the IT department
- the owner is the emotional support hotline

Buyers can't buy this type confidently. They discount it or avoid it.

So, your mission is simple: Make your business look like a Business (Type 1).

7.3 — The Confidence Equation

Confidence comes down to this formula:

Confidence = Proof − Surprises

If buyers see:

- proof of revenue
- proof of customer retention
- proof of SOPs
- proof of clean records
- proof of leadership stability

Confidence rises and risk decreases.

If buyers encounter surprises:

- "Oh, that contract isn't signed"
- "That revenue isn't recurring"
- "That employee is a contractor… but treated like an employee"
- "That customer pays cash sometimes"
- "We don't track that"

Confidence drops and value drops with it.

7.4 — What Buyers Pay Premium Multiples For

Buyers pay extra for businesses that feel stable. Here's what increases confidence fast:

Premium Confidence Builders

1. **Recurring revenue**
2. **Diversified customer base**
3. **Signed contracts**
4. **Strong documentation**
5. **Clean financial reporting**
6. **Management team / #2 leader**
7. **Low operational chaos**
8. **Predictable margins**
9. **Great reputation (reviews, referrals)**
10. **Owner replaceability**

If you're missing some of these, don't panic.

This is not about perfection… It's about improvement.

7.5 — The #1 Buyer Fear: Owner Dependency

If your business depends on you for everything, buyers see it as fragile.

They fear the risk of "Owner Departure."

They think: "The moment the owner leaves, the magic leaves."

Your job is to prove that isn't true.

How to reduce owner dependency (and boost value):

- introduce customers to the team (not just you)
- document processes
- delegate decision-making
- build a leadership layer
- have systems for sales, fulfillment, billing
- remove yourself from daily operations

If you do this well, you'll transform your business from:

"Brilliant owner-run business" into "Transferable asset."

That shift is where valuation jumps happen.

7.6 — Buyers Don't Want Potential. They Want Predictability.

Sellers often say:

- "We could expand"
- "We haven't even tapped that market"
- "If someone just spent more on ads…"

Buyers nod politely but internally think: "If it's so easy, why didn't you do it?"

Buyers don't pay top dollar for:

- untapped markets
- "if we just…" ideas
- vague growth plans

They pay top dollar for:

- proven results
- repeatable systems
- documented performance

Growth potential matters but only if it's credible.

7.7 — The "Confidence Presentation" Position Your Business

A high-confidence sale does not look like:

- seller emailing random PDFs
- searching for documents
- vague explanations
- inconsistent answers

A high-confidence sale looks like:

- organized data room
- clean folder structure
- labeled financials by year/month
- contracts in one place
- customer breakdown available
- policies and SOPs available
- quick responses

Remember: Buyers judge your business by how you handle the sale process.

7.8 — The Buyer's "Trust Scorecard"

Here's a simplified version of what buyers evaluate subconsciously:

Buyer Trust Scorecard

Category	High Confidence
• Financials	• clean, consistent, clear add-backs
• Documentation	• easy to locate, well labeled
• Customers	• stable, diversified, contracts
• Leadership	• team exists beyond owner
• Operations	• SOPs + consistent execution
• Legal	• no surprises, leases/contracts clear
• Culture	• employees stable, not a revolving door

You don't need 10/10 in every category, but the more categories you score high in… the more a buyer feels safe paying premium.

7.9 — The "Confidence Builder Kit" (Easy Wins)

Here are the simplest improvements that increase buyer confidence:

Confidence Kit

1. **Monthly financial packets**
2. **Customer revenue breakdown**
3. **Signed agreements where possible**
4. **Documented SOPs (even if simple)**
5. **Org chart**
6. **Job descriptions**
7. **Vendor list and contracts**
8. **Equipment list**
9. **Insurance summary**
10. **Key metrics dashboard (even basic)**

Buyers love dashboards. Not because dashboards are magic but because dashboards show the owner:

- tracks data
- manages performance
- has control

Control = Confidence
7.10 — The Real "Secret" to Premium Offers

Here's the best sentence in this chapter:

"Buyers pay more for businesses that feel easy to own."

If your business feels like:

- systems do the work
- the team is stable
- customers are locked in
- financials are credible
- documentation is ready

Buyers will:

- compete
- move faster
- accept fewer concessions
- pay more
- push fewer earnouts

But if your business feels like:

- chaos
- undocumented processes

- "figure it out later"
- owner dependency

Buyers will:

- discount
- add restrictions
- demand protections
- delay closing

Your "sales strategy" isn't just marketing… It's operational maturity.

Chapter 7 Summary — The Buyer Isn't Buying Your Business… They're Buying Confidence

"The plans of the diligent end in profit, but those of the hasty end in loss."
— *The Book of Proverbs 21:5*

Confidence Is the Real Product You're Selling

- Your product is not just services.
- Your product is not just equipment.
- Your product is not even revenue.

Your product is a predictable business system that produces earnings.

Confidence is the currency buyers use to decide:

- what they'll pay
- how they'll structure the deal
- how much risk they'll accept

Action Plan: Confidence Checklist

- Identify the top 3 buyer fears in your business
- Reduce owner dependency in one area immediately
- Start by creating a simple SOP for 1 key process
- Build/clean your data room
- Create a basic dashboard (monthly revenue, margin, top customers)
- Have a team member take over 1 buyer-facing relationship

Up Next: Chapter 8 — Deal Killers (and How to Avoid Them)

In Chapter 8, we'll talk about the issues that kill deals at the finish line, and how to prevent them before buyers ever have a chance to panic.

The best strategy to prevent deal killers is simple: Don't give the buyer ammunition.

Chapter 8

Deal Killers (and How to Avoid Them)

"An ounce of prevention is worth a pound of cure."
— BENJAMIN FRANKLIN

If you're looking for the chapter where we talk about unicorn buyers who show up early, offer full price in cash, don't ask for documentation, and close in 30 days…

This is not that chapter. This chapter is about reality.

Deals don't usually die with fireworks… They die quietly.

A deal starts strong:

- buyer is excited
- LOI signed
- due diligence underway
- lawyers exchanging drafts
- everyone is optimistic

Then one day your intermediary calls and says: "The buyer is getting cold feet."

Translation:

- the buyer found risk
- or thinks they found risk
- or wants leverage
- or their spouse talked sense into them
- or their lender got nervous
- or their confidence dropped

Deal killers are anything that:

- breaks trust
- increases perceived risk
- creates chaos
- or makes the buyer feel like they're walking into a trap

Your job is to remove deal killers before the buyer ever sees them. Once a deal killer appears, the buyer does not say: "No worries, we trust you!"

They say: "We need to renegotiate." Which is buyer language for: "We just found the reason to pay you less."

Let's make sure that doesn't happen.

8.1 — Most Deal Killers Are Not "Big Problems"

Here's what surprises most sellers: Deal killers are rarely huge catastrophic disasters.

They are usually small problems that signal:

- disorganization
- lack of control
- lack of transparency

- hidden risk
- or "future headaches"

Buyers are not just buying earnings… They're buying a future.

They want the future to be:

- predictable
- manageable
- boring (in a good way)

Risk is expensive. So, when buyers sense risk, they discount or walk.

8.2 — The Top 10 Deal Killers (and How to Fix Them)

Let's go through the real killers. These are the ones that destroy deals every day.

Deal Killer #1: Inconsistent Financials

What buyers see:
"Revenue is different everywhere. Something doesn't match."

Why it kills deals:
Numbers are trust. If they don't match, trust breaks.

How to fix it:

- reconcile financials monthly
- match tax returns to financial story
- prepare a clear SDE/EBITDA bridge
- document add-backs with receipts

Deal Killer #2: Tax Problems

What buyers see:
Missing returns. Late filings. Tax liens. Aggressive reporting.

Why it kills deals:
Taxes are one of the fastest ways to inherit risk.

How to fix it:

- get all returns filed and organized
- resolve tax issues before sale
- ensure sales tax compliance (especially if applicable)

Deal Killer #3: Customer Concentration

What buyers see:
"Top 1–3 customers are > 50% of revenue."

Why it kills deals:
One customer leaving can destroy earnings.

How to fix it:

- diversify accounts before sale
- secure long-term agreements if possible
- prove retention history
- create customer communication plan post-sale

Deal Killer #4: Owner Dependency

What buyers see:
"This business IS the owner."

Why it kills deals:
Buyers can't buy your personality.

How to fix it:

- build a #2 leader and team
- delegate customer relationships
- document processes
- implement SOPs + training

Deal Killer #5: Poor Documentation

What buyers see:
"We can't find contracts, insurance, leases, employee files…"

Why it kills deals:
It signals poor management and hidden risk.

How to fix it:

- build data room
- label everything clearly
- upload clean versions only
- keep a diligence tracker

Deal Killer #6: Employee Risk

What buyers see:

- key employee might leave
- high turnover
- poor HR documentation
- misclassified contractors

Why it kills deals:
The buyer doesn't want to buy a business and immediately start recruiting.

How to fix it:

- retention plan for key staff
- clear role documentation
- fix contractor classification issues
- implement basic HR policies

Deal Killer #7: Legal Problems or Pending Litigation

What buyers see:

- lawsuits
- threats of lawsuits
- disputes with vendors/customers

Why it kills deals:
Legal risk creates unpredictable future costs.

How to fix it:

- disclose issues early
- resolve disputes if possible before sale
- ensure proper insurance coverage
- get attorney to assess exposure
- ensure leases are assignable

Deal Killer #8: Weak Systems / Outdated IT

What buyers see:

- password chaos
- no process controls
- customer data scattered
- programmer dependent software
- "the business runs on sticky notes"

Why it kills deals:

Operational risk + cybersecurity + inefficiency = deal drag.

How to fix it:

- centralize systems
- document software stack
- build access controls
- create "IT handoff package"

Deal Killer #9: Inventory and Equipment Confusion

What buyers see:

- outdated inventory records
- unclear equipment ownership
- missing titles or liens

Why it kills deals:

Buyers don't want to pay for assets they can't verify.

How to fix it:

- inventory audit
- equipment list
- lien verification
- asset documentation

Deal Killer #10: The Seller's Behavior

Yes, you can kill your own deal.

What buyers see:

- slow responses
- defensiveness
- refusing to share info
- "I'm too busy"
- emotional reactions

Why it kills deals:

Buyers assume this is how ownership will be: difficult.

How to fix it:

- stay calm
- respond quickly
- let intermediary manage tension
- do not negotiate in anger

8.3 — "Closing Creep" Can Be a Deal Killer

This is when:

- the buyer keeps adding new requests
- attorneys keep adding new clauses
- timelines keep slipping
- everybody gets tired

It's death by 1,000 paper cuts. The buyer isn't always being malicious... Sometimes they're just nervous.

The Fix:

- keep deadlines
- keep deal momentum
- track open items
- resolve issues quickly
- don't let attorneys "debate philosophy"

8.4 — The "Prevention Plan": Build a Deal-Proof Business

Here's how smart sellers prevent deal killers:

Deal-Proof Plan

1. **Clean books (reconciled, consistent)**
2. **Document everything (data room)**
3. **Remove owner dependency**
4. **Reduce customer concentration**
5. **Fix HR classification and key staff risks**
6. **Stabilize contracts/leases**

7. **Close legal and tax loose ends**
8. **Run a professional process**

If you do these things, you will not just avoid deal killers... You will raise your valuation.

Low risk = premium multiple.

8.5 — Quick "Deal Risk Scoreboard" (Simple for Buyers and Sellers)

This is a simple internal tool. Rate yourself 1–5 on each category:

Deal Risk Factor	Score (1=high risk, 5=low risk)
• Clean financials	_____
• Tax compliance	_____
• Customer diversification	_____
• Contracts in place	_____
• Lease stability	_____
• Team stability	_____
• Systems documented	_____
• Legal exposure	_____

If any category is a 1 or 2, fix it before listing. That's the cheapest way to increase value.

Chapter 8 Summary — Deal Killers (and How to Avoid Them)

"**Success depends upon previous preparation,
and without such preparation there is sure to be failure.**"— *Confucius*

Every deal killer does the same thing: It reduces buyer confidence and reduced confidence leads to:

- lower offers
- worse deal structure
- delays
- or deal death

The best sellers are not perfect… They are prepared.

Action Plan: Deal Killer Checklist

- Identify the top 5 risks in your business *from a buyer perspective*
- Start by fixing 1 "easy" deal killer immediately (documentation, lease, HR files)
- Create a diligence tracker spreadsheet
- Review lease terms and assignability
- Identify customer concentration and build mitigation plan
- Conduct a mini legal/tax review with attorney/CPA
- Build a "no surprises" mindset

Up Next: Chapter 9 — Cash in Your Pocket

In Chapter 9, we'll talk about the part sellers care about most:

How much money you actually keep!

Because a $10 million sale doesn't mean much if you only walk away with $6 million.

Believe me… A lot of sellers learn that too late.

Chapter 9

Cash in Your Pocket

"A dollar today is worth more than a dollar tomorrow."
— Benjamin Franklin

Let's have a real conversation.

When business owners say: "I sold my business for $10 million."

That sounds like a mic-drop moment.

But what they *really mean* is:

"The purchase price was $10 million... before taxes... before fees... before debt payoff... before working capital adjustments... before earnouts... before escrow... before the buyer got nervous."

In other words:

The sale price is a headline... Cash in your pocket is the truth!

This chapter is about the most important question in the whole process:

How much money do you actually walk away with?

Not in theory. Not on paper. In real life.

9.1 — The Sale Price Illusion

Let's make this simple.

Two deals can have the same purchase price... and wildly different cash outcomes.

Deal A:

- **Price: $10,000,000**
- Professional fees: -$800,000
- Seller note: -$0
- Earnout: -$0
- **Est. net cash before tax at closing: $9,800,000**

Deal B:

- **Purchase price: $10,000,000**
- Professional fees: -$800,000
- Debt payoff: -$700,000
- Working capital adjustment: -$350,000
- Seller note: -$1,000,000 over 3 years
- Earnout: -$2,000,000 tied to performance
- Escrow: $200,000 for 12 months
- **Estimated net cash before tax at closing: $4.950,000**
- (potential for additional $3.2 million over time)

Which deal would you rather have?

- **Sellers** pick Deal A because they want certainty.
- **Buyers** push for Deal B because they want protection.

The final structure depends on:

- risk

- trust
- financial proof
- your leverage
- your willingness to stay involved

Your job is to stop negotiating "price" and start negotiating your net proceeds.

9.2 — The "Net Proceeds" Formula (What You Actually Keep)

Here's the formula buyers never put in the LOI:

Net Proceeds = Purchase Price

Minus:

- debt payoff
- working capital adjustments
- transaction fees
- legal and accounting costs
- broker/intermediary fees
- taxes
- escrow/holdback amounts
- earnouts
- seller note payment (collected over time)
- post-close adjustments

What's left is what hits your bank account.

9.3 — The 7 Biggest Things That Reduce Cash in Your Pocket

1) Taxes

Taxes are usually the #1 bite, but are heavily dependent on:

- deal structure
- asset sale vs stock sale
- allocation of purchase price
- depreciation recapture
- state taxes
- capital gains

We'll cover structure in a simple way soon, but for now:

If you don't plan for taxes early, you'll plan for them too late.

And "late" is expensive.

2) Working Capital Adjustments

This is where sellers get surprised at closing. Example:

- Purchase price: $10M
- Working capital target: $800K
- Actual working capital: $450K
- Difference: Buyer reduces purchase price by: $350K

3) Broker / M&A Fees

Most intermediaries charge:

- 4% to 12% depending on deal size/type
- sometimes with minimums

- sometimes with retainer + success fee

That fee is well earned if they:

- increase valuation
- create buyer competition
- improve structure

4) Attorney + CPA fees

A real business sale has real professional fees.

If your deal involves complexity, you could easily spend:

- $50K – $150K+ in legal
- $45K – $100K+ in accounting support

More if it's larger and this is normal. If you try to "cheap out" here, you'll pay later.

Well-prepared sellers often budget six figures for legal and accounting. Unprepared sellers should budget for more.

The quiet truth is sellers who try to "save" $50K on prep often lose more than 10% - 20% on price or terms.

A strong team of advisors do not just close deals. They reduce buyer fear, shorten diligence, and protect your valuation.

5) Debt Payoff

If the business has:

- equipment loans
- SBA loans

- lines of credit
- vehicles financed

Those get paid off at closing.

So, your "$10M sale" may really be:

$10M – $700K debt = $9.3M before taxes

This is why sellers should know exactly:

- what liens exist
- what payoff numbers are
- whether debt is assumable

6) Seller Notes

Seller notes reduce cash at close but may increase total value.

They can work well… but only if:

- buyer is creditworthy
- terms are strong
- security exists
- payment schedule is enforceable

Otherwise, it becomes: "Congrats on your sale… now pray for a payment every month."

7) Earnouts

Earnouts are the most emotionally dangerous structure for sellers.

Because once the deal closes:

- you often have less control
- the buyer runs operations
- numbers can change
- expenses can be reclassified
- goals can be missed

Earnouts are not always bad, but they should be:

- clearly defined
- measurable
- tied to metrics you can influence
- protected from manipulation

And ideally…

Earnouts should be bonus upside… not core value.

If your "price" depends on an earnout, you didn't really sell yet.

9.4 — Asset Sale vs Stock Sale

This is one of the biggest tax and liability issues.

Asset Sale

The buyer purchases:

- equipment
- inventory
- customer lists
- contracts
- goodwill
- intellectual property

They do NOT buy the company entity itself.

- Common in small business sales
- Buyer-friendly (limits buyer liability)
    - Seller may face higher taxes depending on allocation

Stock Sale (or membership interest sale for LLC)

The buyer purchases the legal entity.

- Seller-friendly in many cases
- Often better capital gains treatment
    - Buyer inherits liabilities, so they may resist

Most small deals are asset sales. Bigger deals may be stock sales.

Your CPA/accountant and attorney should guide you.

9.5 — Allocation of Purchase Price (Hidden Tax Weapon)

Even in an asset sale, the purchase price gets allocated. This allocation can dramatically affect taxes. Common allocation categories:

- cash
- inventory
- equipment
- goodwill
- non-compete

Here's the rule:

Buyers want allocation that benefits them.

- Example: More allocation to equipment (depreciation) and inventory

Sellers want allocation that benefits them.

- Example: More allocation to goodwill (capital gains)

This allocation must be negotiated because it impacts what you keep.

9.6 — The "Cash at Close" Mindset

If you want the safest deal outcome:

Prioritize cash at close.

Cash at close reduces:

- buyer future performance risk
- collection risk
- legal disputes later
- stress

A high-cash deal is a high-confidence deal, and you earn that confidence by:

- clean financials
- documented operations
- low risk profile
- buyer competition

Cash at close is the reward for preparation.

9.7 — The Closing Statement: Where Reality Shows Up

At closing, you'll get a statement with a breakdown.

This is where sellers go:

- "Wait, what's that fee?"

- "What's that adjustment?"
- "What's that payoff?"
- "Why is the escrow so high?"
- "How much do I really get at closing?"

Don't wait until closing to understand the math.

You should create a Net Proceeds forecast early.

It might shock you, but shock is good now. Shock is bad at closing.

9.8 — After the Sale: Don't Blow It

Now let's talk about the part nobody tells sellers:

The sale is not the finish line. It's the start of a new phase.

Many owners are great at building a business, but they are not prepared to manage sudden liquidity.

Common mistakes:

- overbuying assets quickly (cars, boats, toys)
- investing in "friend opportunities"
- lending money to family
- jumping into risky investments
- failing to plan taxes
- feeling lost and spending to feel productive

That's why Chapter 10 will matter so much.

But for this chapter, remember: The goal isn't to sell and celebrate.

The goal is to sell well and stay wealthy.

Chapter 9 Summary — Cash in Your Pocket

"It's not what you earn, it's what you keep." — *Warren Buffett*

Don't Fall in Love with the Purchase Price

A big number on paper means nothing if:

- taxes eat it
- structure delays it
- earnouts make it uncertain
- seller notes make it risky

The diligent seller plans in advance and focuses on:

- net proceeds
- cash at closing
- tax strategy
- deal protection

A planned exit is not just selling the business. It's keeping the money.

Action Plan: Net Proceeds Checklist

- Create a Net Proceeds forecast
- Identify all debts/liens and payoff estimates
- Review working capital definition early
- Discuss taxes with CPA before LOI negotiation
- Negotiate allocation strategically
- Don't accept earnouts unless terms are clear
- Prioritize cash at close (or reduce risk with protections)

Up Next: Chapter 10 — What's My Why?

This is the chapter that makes this book different.

Because selling your business isn't just a financial decision.

It's a life decision.

And once the deal closes, the most important question becomes:

Now what?

Chapter 10

What's My Why?

"There is an appointed time for everything, and a time for every affair under the heavens."
— BOOK OF ECCLESIASTES 3:1

If you're reading this chapter, you're either:

1. Seriously thinking about selling your business, or
2. Already in the middle of it and realizing it's not just paperwork and bank wires… it's emotional.

Because selling a business isn't just a transaction… It's a life transition.

For many owners, it's the first time in decades they've asked a question that isn't about cash flow, payroll, or next quarter:

Why do I want to sell?

Not what you'll get. Not what you're tired of. Not what the business is worth.

But why you're doing it and what comes next?

I'll tell you something most people won't…

Selling your business doesn't automatically create happiness.

It creates options and options are powerful… but only if you choose wisely.

Otherwise, you can sell the business and still feel trapped, restless, or empty.

So, this final chapter is about purpose. It's about identity. It's about what to do with your time, your skills, your money, and your leadership after the deal closes.

It's about making sure you don't just exit your business well… you exit into a meaningful life.

10.1 — The Big Surprise After the Sale: "Now What?"

Here's what many owners don't expect:

The day after the sale often feels weird.

Not bad… Just weird.

You wake up and:

- no emergencies
- no meetings
- no staff questions
- no urgent fires to put out
- no customer drama

Your phone is quiet, and after years of chaos, quiet can feel like peace… or like emptiness.

A lot of business owners think they want freedom, but what they really want is freedom with purpose.

Because without purpose, freedom becomes boredom and boredom becomes regret.

So, let's make sure you plan for what comes next.

10.2 — The Real Reasons People Sell (And All of Them Are Valid)

Most sellers have more than one reason. Here are the most common ones:

1. **You're burned out**
You've been carrying the weight too long, and you want your life back.

2. **You're ready for retirement**
You want peace, family time, travel, hobbies.

3. **Health or family issues**
Sometimes life forces the decision.

4. **You've hit a ceiling**
You know what it would take to scale, and you don't want to do it.

5. **The timing is right**
You're getting strong offers, and you don't want to miss your window.

6. **You want a new challenge**
You're a builder, not a maintainer.

7. **You want to cash out for security**
You want to protect what you've built and lock in wealth.

Every one of these reasons is legitimate, and your reason matters because it influences:

- the type of buyer you choose
- how much transition you're willing to do
- what deal structure works for you
- what success actually looks like

10.3 — The Seller Identity Problem (Nobody Warns You About)

Let's be honest.

For many owners, the business wasn't just income. It was:

- status
- identity
- purpose
- routine
- relationships
- pride
- belonging

When someone says: "What do you do?" - You answer with the business.

After the sale, that disappears, and many sellers go through a quiet "identity withdrawal."

Not because they miss stress but because they miss being needed.

Here's the good news: You don't stop being a leader when you sell.

You just stop having a place to put your leadership… until you choose one.

10.4 — The 4 Paths After You Sell

Most business owners land on one of four paths.

There's no "best." Only what's best *for you*.

Path 1: Retirement

Retirement can be incredible, but retirement doesn't mean "doing nothing." It means:

- choosing your time
- protecting your health
- enjoying family
- living intentionally

Retirement can be the first time you truly breathe.

But here's the trap: Too much leisure without meaning becomes restlessness.

Golf every day sounds fun… until you realize you're playing golf to avoid feeling aimless.

Path 2: Second Career

Some people sell their business and start something new. Not because they need money but because they still want to build.

This path often looks like:

- consulting
- advisory work
- part-time executive roles
- teaching/coaching
- community involvement
- corporate leadership role

Second career works best when:

- It's chosen, not forced
- It's aligned with your strengths
- It gives purpose without consuming your life

Path 3: Investor / Owner

Many sellers become:

- angel investors
- franchise owners
- real estate investors
- buyers of smaller businesses

Warning: Do not become "an investor" just because you sold.

Being an operator and being an investor are different skills.

- Operating is control.
- Investing is patience.

If you go this route, have guidance, do your research, and start slow.

Path 4: Legacy / Service

This is the most fulfilling path for many sellers. It includes:

- mentoring entrepreneurs
- serving on boards
- supporting nonprofits
- civic leadership
- volunteer teacher
- helping veterans, youth programs, workforce development

This path gives the seller something priceless: Purpose without pressure.

It lets you take everything you learned and turn it into impact.

That brings us to one of the most powerful parts of selling a business: You now have the chance to give back.

10.5 — Giving Back: The Highest ROI You'll Ever Get

"**As each one has received a gift, use it to serve one another as good stewards of God's varied grace.**"— *First Epistle of Peter 4:10*

You've built skills most people never develop:

- leadership
- discipline
- systems thinking
- negotiation
- resilience
- decision-making under pressure

That knowledge is valuable beyond business.

When you donate money, it helps… but when you donate leadership and time, it transforms communities.

Examples of how sellers give back:

- mentor new business owners
- seek volunteer opportunities
- sponsor youth programs
- create scholarships
- join nonprofit boards
- lead fundraising campaigns
- support local workforce training and education

The beauty is you can now contribute to what you are passionate about. That's a gift.

10.6 — The "Perfect Exit" Isn't Necessarily the Perfect Deal

Let's redefine success. A perfect exit is not:

- squeezing every last dollar out of the buyer
- bragging about the multiple or the amount
- posting a "humbled and grateful" LinkedIn announcement

A perfect exit is:

- your family is secure
- your stress is lower
- your time becomes yours again
- your health improves
- your mind is clear
- your future feels exciting

A great sale gives you something that's hard to price: Peace and that's priceless.

10.7 — Your Post-Sale Plan (The Practical Version)

Let's bring this home. You need a plan before the sale closes… Not after.

The "Next Chapter" Plan

Here are the 7 things you should define:

1. **How will you spend your first 90 days after closing?**
   Rest? Travel? Heal? Reset?
2. **What does a great week look like?**
   How many days are structured vs free?

3. **What relationships will you invest in?**
   Family? Friends? Community? Church?
4. **What will you build next (if anything)?**
   Business? Investor? Charity? Project?
5. **What will you do for health?**
   Fitness? Checkups? Sleep? Nutrition?
6. **How will you give back?**
   Board Seat? Mentor? Volunteer? Philanthropist?
7. **How will you protect the money?**
   Financial Advisor? Tax Planning? Attorney? Discipline?

Everyone's path is different, but you'll want to turn your freedom into fulfillment.

10.8 — The Final Truth: You're Not Selling Your Business

You're not just selling a business. You're selling:

- responsibility
- pressure
- stress
- identity
- routine

And you're buying:

- time
- flexibility
- peace
- possibility

That's why this moment matters. Because you only get one chance to exit well.

Chapter 10 Summary — What's My Why?

"**What profit is there for one to gain the whole world and forfeit his life?**"
— *Gospel of Mark 8:36*

Exit With Intention

Selling your business is a major milestone, but it shouldn't be the end of your story.

It should be the start of a more meaningful chapter:

- one with purpose
- one with impact
- one with leadership used differently
- one with time and health restored
- one where you get to give back

Because the truth is: Your community needs experienced leaders.

And you have that experience. Not from books… but from real life.

Action Plan: "What's it Worth!" Summary Checklist

- clean financials + tax returns
- realistic valuation
- trustworthy professional team
- due diligence preparation
- negotiation strategy
- protection from deal killers
- clear net proceeds plan
- post-sale life plan

Closing Thought

If you've built a business worth selling, you've already done something extremely rare.

By following this plan and you won't just sell your business… You'll finish strong!

Not just with money… but with meaning.

"Well done, good and faithful servant."
— *Gospel of Matthew 25:21*

APPENDIX

Exit Action Plan Summary

Chapter 1 — Begin with the End in Mind
Action Plan: No More Excuses

Start with these 7 Steps:

- Write down your target exit year
- Decide whether you want cash out, earnout, partial exit, or combination
- Estimate your "number" (how much you want after taxes)
- Identify the 3 biggest risks in your business
- List what only YOU do today
- Choose 1 task to delegate immediately
- Commit to treating your business like an asset — not a job

Chapter 2 — Who Can I Trust?
Action Plan: Build the Team Before You Need the Team

- Identify 2–3 candidates for each core role (Attorney, CPA, Advisor, Intermediary)
- Interview them – Do they pass your Trust Test?
- Ask for references
- Choose your intermediary carefully, because they will drive the process

Chapter 3 — Surviving Due Diligence
Action Plan: Due Diligence Prep

- Create your data room (basic folder structure)
- Upload last 3 years of tax returns
- Upload last 2 years of financial statements
- Pull your top customer list by revenue
- Gather all major contracts
- Create a basic equipment list
- Create an employee roster (name, role, pay, start date)
- Identify your 3 biggest business risks before the buyer does

Chapter 4 — Numbers Don't Lie
Action Plan: Financial Prep Checklist

- Pull last 3 years of tax returns
- Pull year-to-date P&L and balance sheet
- Create monthly P&L statements for last 12–24 months
- Create a clear add-backs list with documentation
- Identify financial inconsistencies before the buyer does
- Clean up personal expenses in business accounts
- Talk with your CPA/accountant about normalization and SDE/EBITDA view

Chapter 5 — Beauty is in the Eye of the Beholder
Action Plan: Valuation Prep Checklist

- Get a baseline valuation range from your intermediary
- Identify what buyer type would pay most for your business

EXIT ACTION PLAN SUMMARY

- List the top 5 value drivers in your company
- List the top 3 risk drivers lowering your multiple
- Decide what's realistic vs what's emotional
- Work with your CPA/accountant to calculate real SDE/EBITDA
- Strengthen documentation and contracts to raise confidence

Chapter 6 — Art of the Deal
Action Plan: Negotiation-Prep Checklist

- Define your minimum acceptable terms (price + structure)
- Create your non-negotiables list
- Make sure your intermediary is running a controlled buyer process
- Avoid single-buyer negotiations if possible
- Prepare for common buyer tactics (push for earnout, holdback, working capital)
- Decide in advance how long you're willing to stay post-close

Chapter 7 — The Buyer Isn't Buying Your Business... They're Buying Confidence
Action Plan: Confidence Checklist

- Identify the top 3 buyer fears in your business
- Reduce owner dependency in one area immediately
- Start by creating a simple SOP for 1 key process
- Build/clean your data room
- Create a basic dashboard (monthly revenue, margin, top customers)
- Have a team member take over 1 buyer-facing relationship

Chapter 8 Summary — Deal Killers (and How to Avoid Them)
Action Plan: Deal Killer Checklist

- Identify the top 5 risks in your business *from a buyer perspective*
- Start by fixing 1 "easy" deal killer immediately (documentation, lease, HR files)
- Create a diligence tracker spreadsheet
- Review lease terms and assignability
- Identify customer concentration and build mitigation plan
- Conduct a mini legal/tax review with attorney/CPA
- Build a "no surprises" mindset

Chapter 9 Summary — Cash in Your Pocket
Action Plan: Net Proceeds Checklist

- Create a Net Proceeds forecast
- Identify all debts/liens and payoff estimates
- Review working capital definition early
- Discuss taxes with CPA before LOI negotiation
- Negotiate allocation strategically
- Don't accept earnouts unless terms are clear
- Prioritize cash at close (or reduce risk with protections)

Chapter 10 Summary — What's My Why?
Action Plan: Create your next meaningful chapter:

- One with purpose
- One with impact
- One with leadership used differently

- One with time and health restored
- One where you get to give back

Summary — What's it Worth!
Action Plan: Exit with Intention

- clean financials + tax returns
- realistic valuation
- trustworthy professional team
- due diligence preparation
- negotiation strategy
- protect against deal killers
- clear net proceeds plan
- post-sale life plan

About the Author

Michael Toups

What's It Worth? is drawn from decades of experience on both sides of the negotiating table. Michael has worked alongside buyers, sellers, bankers, boards, and entrepreneurs to answer the questions that ultimately drive every exit transaction: what is a business truly worth, and how do you maximize value before you sell?

Michael is a seasoned executive, investment banker, and operator with more than 30 years of experience leading, buying, selling, and scaling companies in the U.S. and abroad. He began his career in corporate banking and transitioned into boutique investment banking, where he advised business owners on mergers and acquisitions, capital formation, and transaction strategy.

Beyond his executive roles, Michael has served as a board-level advisor to portfolio companies, helping leadership teams refine strategy, strengthen operations, and prepare for liquidity events. He has also advised business owners on expansion into the public sector and government marketplace.

As an entrepreneur, Michael brings firsthand experience to the exit process. He has successfully exited four startup ventures over the course of his career. While each exit had its own unique challenges, each one provided practical insights into valuation, deal structure, negotiations, due diligence, and the personal dynamics involved in selling a business. Those real-world experiences, both the wins and the challenges, shape the practical guidance shared in this book.

Michael holds an MBA in Finance from the University of Notre Dame, a BBA in Finance from Texas Christian University, and a Higher Education Teaching Certificate from Harvard University.

https://www.linkedin.com/in/michaeltoups

For more information visit: *www.WhatsItWorthConsult.com*